I0509661

This 2020 Sketchbook
Belongs To:

______________________________

Drawing Pad
Blank Paper Press


Contact: DrawingPadPress@gmail.com

www.ingramcontent.com/pod-product-compliance
Lightning Source LLC
Chambersburg PA
CBHW080605220526
45466CB00010B/3255
* 9 7 8 1 6 5 5 3 7 9 9 9 4 *